GRAHAM OF
THRONES

GRAHAM OF THRONES

A PARODY

GRAHAM R. R. STARK

SIMON &
SCHUSTER

London · New York · Sydney · Toronto · New Delhi

A CBS COMPANY

First published in Great Britain by Simon & Schuster UK Ltd, 2014
A CBS company

3 5 7 9 10 8 6 4 2

Simon & Schuster UK Ltd
1st Floor
222 Gray's Inn Road
London WC1X 8HB

www.simonandschuster.co.uk

Simon & Schuster Australia, Sydney

Simon & Schuster India, New Delhi

Every reasonable effort has been made to contact copyright holders
of material reproduced in this book. If any have inadvertently been
overlooked, the publishers would be glad to hear from them and make
good in future editions any errors or omissions brought to their attention.

A CIP catalogue record for this book is available from the British Library

ISBN: 978-1-47114-164-5

Ebook ISBN: 978-1-47114-165-2

Typeset and designed in the UK by Nick Venables

Printed and bound in Spain by Graficas Estella

For Charles Hawtrey,
the original lavatory man.

PRACTICAL PLUMBING FOR PROFESSIONALS

1ST EDITION

BY CHARLES STARK

My father shook me awake and soon we ventured out into the cold winter dawn. 'The time has come, Graham my lad. Time to prove that you are a man!'

I rode alongside him in his rickety old van, excited but nervous. What trial was I expected to perform on this, my eighteenth birthday? Before I knew what was happening, we had reached our destination and he was beckoning me to his side.

'You need to understand, son, that sometimes a man has no choice but to take the most extreme measures. When a problem can't be fixed, there is only one course of action left. To remove the head. Now I want you to watch carefully.'

I nodded.

'And don't look away. I will know if you do.'

I shook my head and stared steadfastly forward.

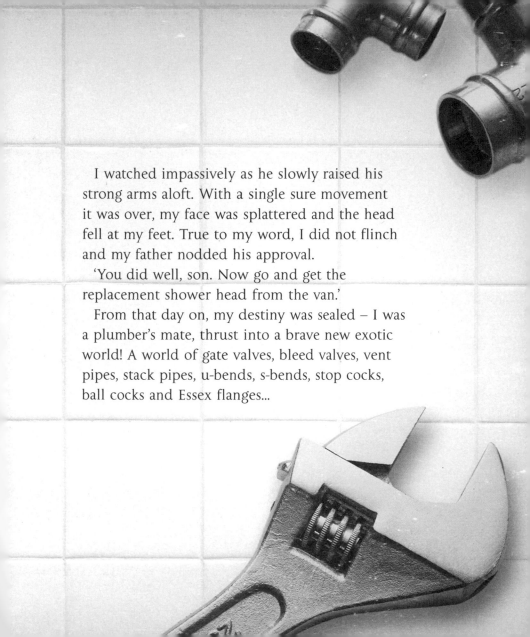

I watched impassively as he slowly raised his strong arms aloft. With a single sure movement it was over, my face was splattered and the head fell at my feet. True to my word, I did not flinch and my father nodded his approval.

'You did well, son. Now go and get the replacement shower head from the van.'

From that day on, my destiny was sealed – I was a plumber's mate, thrust into a brave new exotic world! A world of gate valves, bleed valves, vent pipes, stack pipes, u-bends, s-bends, stop cocks, ball cocks and Essex flanges...

I stared in horror –
it was a dark, evil green
colour with big scales.

I hadn't seen a bathroom
like this since 1973.

'I like it rough,'
she said, bending
over the hand basin.
'How about you?'

I stared hard at her.
'Actually I prefer
quilted toilet paper.'

She closed her long fingers around the end and tugged gently. Then harder. 'Why isn't anything happening?' she asked, disappointed.

'Sorry,' I said. 'It only works on the third flush.'

'You are my hero!'
she cried.

'It was nothing,' I answered.
'I'm from Leeds.
I'm used to holding a
woman's hair while
she throws up.'

As I gazed up at the
stars, giant mystical balls
of flaming bright light that
shape our destiny with
their vast cosmic dance,
a thought came to me –
I really must fix the roof
on this outdoor loo.

I lay the manual down on my lap and sigh heavily. Why would anyone lock me in my own bathroom? And on such an auspicious day, too. How long have I been in here? Normally, with a wife and four kids, I don't get more than two minutes in here. If only they were here now, they could let me out. I blame that weird TV show everyone's banging on about these days. What's it called now, Game of something or other?

Ever since she started watching it, she's been completely obsessed – with dragons mostly. She's got a dragon jumper, a dragon necklace, a dragon teapot, a set of limited edition dragon pasta dishes, a life-size inflatable dragon and even a dragon tattoo on her inner thigh. Apparently. And now she's gone and taken the kids off to Dragonland for a week!

And on top of that, there's all that gratuitous sex and violence. But I suppose I knew about that when I married her. Things are getting so bad, I'm beginning to lose track of the difference between fantasy and reality myself...

I fell to my knees
as she showed me her vast
array of brightly coloured
baby dragons. Never again
would I let my wife loose
in a Welsh craft fair.

I gazed upon the ring.
It told of rain-drenched
journeys, it told of mud-sodden
conflicts – but most of
all it told me my bloody
son hadn't cleaned the bath
after using it again!

We stood in solemn reverence as yet another of our friends was transported to his watery grave.

Colin was the third goldfish we'd had to flush down the toilet that month.

As the pain surged up my body, I swore terrible vengeance. How many times have I told my son not to leave his Lego on the bathroom floor?

'Go, my brave warrior!'
came her trembling voice from
afar. 'We all have faith in you!'

'That's all very well,' I said.
'But have you seen the size
of that spider?'

She dropped her skirt,
pulled down her panties
and slowly lowered
herself onto my lap.

I really must get a new
light bulb for this toilet.

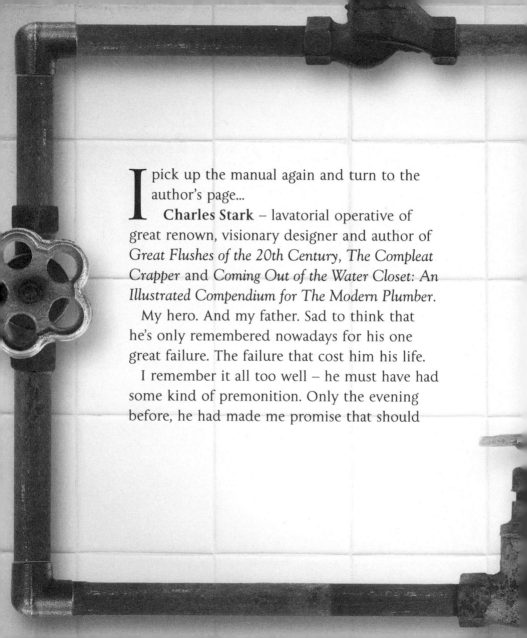

I pick up the manual again and turn to the author's page...

Charles Stark – lavatorial operative of great renown, visionary designer and author of *Great Flushes of the 20th Century*, *The Compleat Crapper* and *Coming Out of the Water Closet: An Illustrated Compendium for The Modern Plumber*.

My hero. And my father. Sad to think that he's only remembered nowadays for his one great failure. The failure that cost him his life.

I remember it all too well – he must have had some kind of premonition. Only the evening before, he had made me promise that should anything happen to him, I would continue his ground-breaking work for the Society of Drainage, Overflow Management and Incorporated Toilet Engineers.

He was so dedicated, he never missed a single meeting. I'll never forget the cheery wink he used to give my mother when he went off to the Ilkley Grand Hotel for yet another weekend with his fellow Sodomites. My only hope is that he felt no pain in the end. And my only consolation is the knowledge that he never saw his only son fail to continue his legacy...

I was horrified that
one woman's decision
could lead to such an
appalling, violent clash.

A salmon-pink toilet
with an avocado
hand basin?

I screamed in agony as the heat stung my naked flesh, 'How many times have I told you not to flush the toilet when I'm in the shower?'

With a heavy heart,
I realised that I was sixth
in line to the throne.
I had two choices, I could
slay the five others
before me . . . or go
behind a tree.

I sat in quiet contemplation for several minutes before my reverie was shattered by a ghastly vision emerging from the watery depths.

Next time I use the toilet, I'll check my mother-in-law isn't in the bath first.

I gasped as the egg split
slowly open and out poked
a small green snout, then
two bright red eyes and a pair
of spiked, leathery wings.
There's no doubt about it,
these Kinder Surprises really
live up to their name.

As my mind slowly returns to my current predicament, the manual falls open at another page and I am transported back to a summer evening when Barbara put her arms lovingly around me, gently kissed my neck and whispered, 'Graham, I think it's time we moved to the next stage.' And then came those evocative little French words . . . en-suite.

Six months later, the nights had drawn in. We'd moved to the next stage and Barbara had her en-suite. That was the winter of the Great Flood.

'I'm not happy, Graham!'

I could tell by the look on my wife's face that there was something on her mind. 'Your plumbing business is going down the tubes, the bills are piling up and now I need a dinghy to get to the bidet! I keep telling you, we've got to leave the North, there's more money down in Essex.'

Typical Barbara! Ever since we got engaged, she'd been trying to get me to go down South. Up till now I'd managed to get away with only going as far as the Midlands – and then it was just for her birthday.

The journey South was to prove a long, tortuous trek. We set off in my plumber's van, full of hope, down the Tadcaster Road at the crack of dawn. Everything was going smoothly until the van caught fire on the M1 near Northampton. After two hours of Barbara hitching up her skirt on the slip road and me hitching up my trousers, we finally got a lift to the nearest train station.

Who would have thought a Nissan Micra could fit a family of six and their pull-out sofa bed? It wasn't easy for Barbara standing on the train with our luggage and kids, but, as I pointed out, I had to have the last seat due to my plumber's knee, plumber's back and plumber's groin.

After negotiating the last ten miles from the station on foot, we finally arrived at our new home as night fell. I couldn't believe my eyes! What wondrous place was this? Perhaps Barbara had been right about Essex all along! The houses were like palaces – blinds instead of curtains, floodlit drives, immaculate lawns and more fountains than the Ideal Water Feature Exhibition. Wester Ross Close!

SEA
THE NORTH
TADCASTER
CARPET WORLD
THE MIDLANDS
NORTHAMPTON
DRAGONLAND
ESSEX
LEGOLAND
BLUEWATER
CHANNEL
ENGLISH CHANNEL

The procession of weary travellers stretched as far as the eye could see, edging slowly forward. Desperate and hopeless, some fell by the wayside with exhaustion while others clung on for dear life, not knowing how long their tormented quest would continue.

Motorway service toilet queues are getting ridiculous these days.

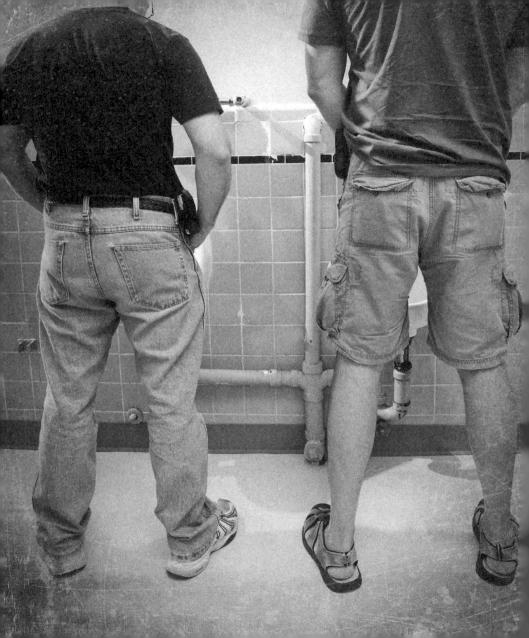

We stood there, shoulder to shoulder, staring defiantly ahead. Looking anywhere else would be completely inappropriate at a urinal.

After hours of blood-curdling screams and groans, he emerged breathless and said, 'I wouldn't go in there for a few minutes if I were you.'

Alone and desperate,
I crouched in the gloom
and whistled nervously.
There's nothing more
terrifying than a toilet
door without a lock . . .

Whenever I've been on
the toilet for a while, my
wife always starts banging
on the bathroom door.

Eventually it gets so
annoying I have to
let her out.

Please
don't flush

**Nappies, sanitary towels,
paper towels, gum,
old phones, unpaid bills
junk mail, your ex's sweater,
hopes, dreams or goldfish**

down this
toilet

As I was frogmarched away by a pair of hulking guards, I was acutely aware of the consequence of my foolish action. I should never have flushed the toilet while the train was in the station.

Having read my father's manual from cover to cover for the sixth time, I stare at the immovable bathroom door and feel myself beginning to panic. Though not as much as I did twelve months ago, when I heard my wife calling from the kitchen.

'Graham! Graham! Get out of that toilet and get down those stairs!'

I sighed, pulled up my jeans and reluctantly headed out to face my greatest fear, the thing that struck terror into my very soul – a Housewarming Party. With Southerners.

The bottles were lined up, the egg and cress sandwiches stood to attention, and the sausage rolls readied for the ensuing melee. Then after a short, uneasy calm, battle commenced. The cheese and pineapple chunks were speared, the satay chicken skewered, the flesh torn from the drumsticks, the brie and broccoli quiche sliced and the cocktail sausages impaled.

Almost as soon as it had started, the scene was a devastated wasteland, littered with the ravages of conflict. And then all fell silent. It was always so hard knowing what to say at these things.

My memory of the rest of the evening is a little hazy, thanks to the bottle of Chateau Lafite Jeremy and Selena brought and the magnum of Cristal Karl and Delandra provided. Although I do have a vague recollection of entertaining everyone with my holiday snaps...

The next thing I remember was waking up, with my head resting on the toilet seat and a Spring Blossom rim freshener rammed up against my nose. Barbara was surprisingly understanding about the whole thing – although, as she pointed out, if I must force a room full of new acquaintances to watch a slideshow of holiday photos, it might be a little more entertaining if they weren't all of toilets.

Eventually, after my fifth Alka Seltzer, she told me all about our new next-door neighbours. How Jeremy was terribly big in bathrooms and Karl was terribly big everywhere, being a professional rugby player. And also how understanding he was, even after finding my hand up his wife's hairy jumper. Barbara seemed certain that we would fit in perfectly in Wester Ross Close, but I wasn't quite so sure...

I took in the sweet aroma
of the morning dew on the
mountain flowers and the
fresh summer breeze of the
fjords and sighed wistfully.

This Nordic Sunrise air
freshener certainly
did the job.

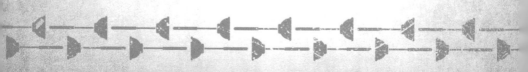

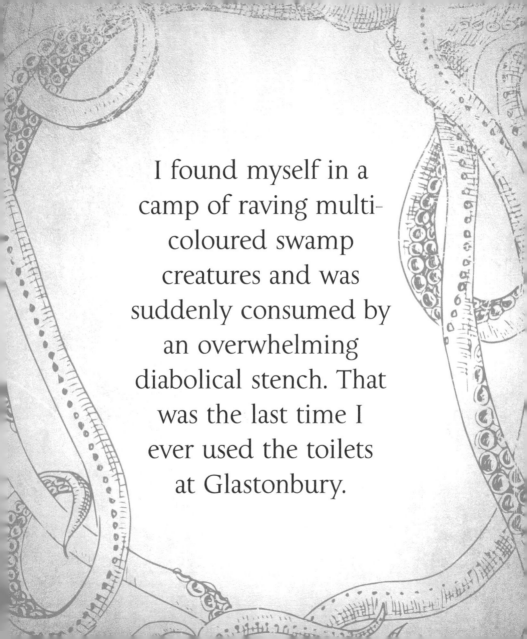

I found myself in a camp of raving multi-coloured swamp creatures and was suddenly consumed by an overwhelming diabolical stench. That was the last time I ever used the toilets at Glastonbury.

After climbing down the steep stone steps and pushing open the ancient creaking door, I crossed the leathery outstretched palm of the gnarled old woman in black with several pieces of silver. But she still gave me only one small square of toilet paper.

TOILE

2 POUND ←

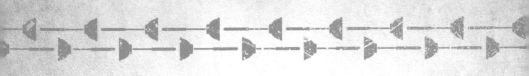

It was the day of my initiation.
I had heard many myths and legends
about what I would endure, but few
had lived to tell the tale. Trembling
with fear, I pulled back the heavy gate
and entered. And there it was – the
sight and stench of the evil Black Hole
was even more fearsome than I had
imagined! It was the first time I'd
used a French campsite toilet and
it would definitely be the last!

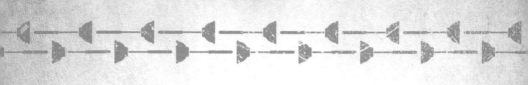

I swiped vigorously and manfully, hard and fast, up and down and side to side, but despite all my efforts I was still defeated. That's shiny toilet paper for you.

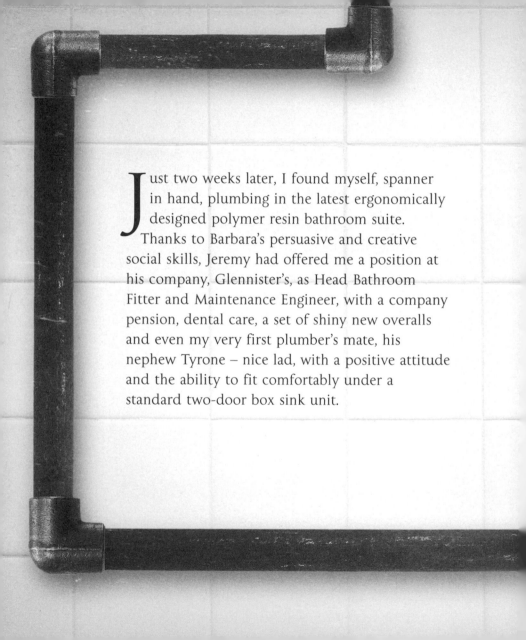

Just two weeks later, I found myself, spanner in hand, plumbing in the latest ergonomically designed polymer resin bathroom suite.
Thanks to Barbara's persuasive and creative social skills, Jeremy had offered me a position at his company, Glennister's, as Head Bathroom Fitter and Maintenance Engineer, with a company pension, dental care, a set of shiny new overalls and even my very first plumber's mate, his nephew Tyrone – nice lad, with a positive attitude and the ability to fit comfortably under a standard two-door box sink unit.

It was a source of great pride that I was able to take him under my wing, just as my own father had done with me all those years ago. I even offered him my father's manual but, as he said, 'Books are good, but a bacon sandwich is better.'

He was full of funny little sayings like that: 'Too many cooks spoil the bacon', 'Don't put all your bacon in one sandwich' and 'Keep your friends close and your sandwiches closer'. He was clearly a highly focused young man.

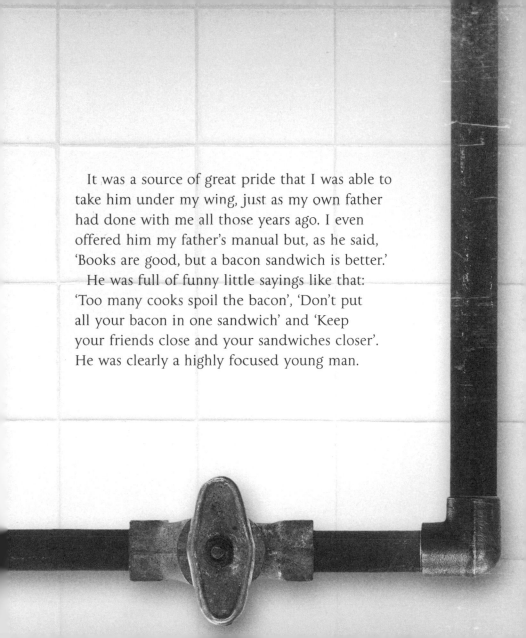

I twisted, turned, kicked, punched and finally head-butted. But I still couldn't work out how to use the taps in these gastro pub toilets.

I raised the vessel and gulped down the demonic brew. It was several swigs before I realised I'd mixed up the Jägermeister with the toilet duck.

The high-born and
well-to-do sat at the top table
devouring their banquet while,
nearby, the peasants fought over
their discarded chicken bones.
Nando's really does cater
for everyone.

I stared at the hellish scene – an orgy of lust amid the carnage of lifeless bodies. Never again would I use an Essex nightclub toilet.

'No!' he said, staring sadly at the burly trucker belting out 'I Am What I Am' in a blonde wig and stilettos. 'I said I wanted to see the DRAGON queen!'

In spite of Tyrone's stimulating company, it wasn't long before I began to find the day-to-day life of a Glennister's Head Bathroom Fitter and Maintenance Engineer wasn't all it was cracked up to be. Sure, it paid the bills and allowed my wife to live in the dragon-infested manner to which she had become accustomed, but I was like a leaky wash basin – unfulfilled. In contrast, Barbara had never been happier, spending her days luxuriating in Delandra's hot tub and popping enthusiastically in and out of Selena's gazebo. I have to admit I had my concerns, but as ever they were allayed by Tyrone's wise words.

'A happy wife is almost as good as a bacon sandwich.'

Then, one fateful Tuesday evening, after a particularly laborious encounter with a troublesome shower unit, I arrived home to find a small yellow note stuck to the oven door: 'Your dinner's in the kids. I'm in Jeremy's golden jacuzzi.'

Tired and hungry, I shrugged my shoulders and rummaged through the cupboards in search of something to satisfy my hunger, but found only a Pot Noodle and a long cardboard tube. Curious, I moved the Pot Noodle aside, pulled out the tube and patted one end. Onto the granite work surface fell a rolled-up A2 sheet of draughtsman's 120 gsm cartridge paper. I smoothed it flat and what I saw both astounded me and brought a tear to my eye.

'The Galvanised Self-unblocking Multi-speed Hyper-suction Turbo-Flush Lavatory'. The Iron Throne! my father's greatest ever achievement – the invention that was to revolutionise the entire plumbing industry. And end his life.

The blueprint trembled in my grip as I recalled that momentous day when he came rushing, wild-eyed, into my mother's kitchen shouting 'Eureka!' I looked up bemused as she tutted and told him to take off his boots and wash his hands before tea. But, too excited to pay her heed, he dashed straight back down into the shed, slamming the door shut behind him.

The next thing we heard there was one flush, a long sequence of loud gurgles, a short pause, then a second flush, an almighty bang and a terrible sucking sound followed by a high-pitched scream. When we finally managed to break down the door, after we'd finished our tea, our eyes were met by the chilling sight of a giant black throne-like machine belching smoke and groaning demonically and not a sign of father, save for a pair of charred hobnail boots standing either side of his erect over-sized plunger.

I wiped my eyes as I stared down at the plans, so meticulously drawn by my father's china blue draughtsman's pencil – what could possibly have gone wrong? Could it have been the integrated thermostat? Or maybe the multi-directional bypass flange? Or possibly...?

I shook my head sharply. What was I thinking? My father was a genius. Who was I, a lowly bathroom fitter, to imagine I could solve this riddle where he had failed?

I swiftly rolled up the blueprint, returned it to its tube and shoved it into my spanner bag, to throw into the bin the next morning. Then I settled down on the sofa with my Pot Noodle and *Midsomer Murders* and thought no more of it.

I slashed wildly as the demented winged creature circled crazily above me.

It wasn't easy peeing straight with a moth in the bathroom.

'I want it now,' she cried. 'I want it long, I want it hard and I want it right up against this wall!'

'All right,' I said. 'But personally, I prefer a free-standing bath.'

I leapt from the battlement on top of one, knocked another out with a roundhouse kick and finally threw the last two over the wall. Then I was asked to get off the bouncy castle.

I stared dumbfounded,
trying to decipher the two
mystical symbols that would
guide my fate. One way would
lead to satisfaction and peace,
the other to shame,
degradation and humiliation.

I do wish they would write
Male and Female on their toilet
doors like everywhere else!

As the crazed, wolf-like
creature surged forward,
causing chaos and carnage,
its master could only stand
there helpless, shouting,
'Fenton! . . . Fenton!!'

Time was running out. As the sun
began to set behind the trees and
nightfall approached, I rowed with
all my might across the lake, dragged
myself through the perilous pit of
sand and climbed, swung and slid
over the many obstacles in my way –
until finally I arrived, exhausted and
desperate, at the heavy iron gates.
But my efforts were in vain –
the park toilets closed at dusk.

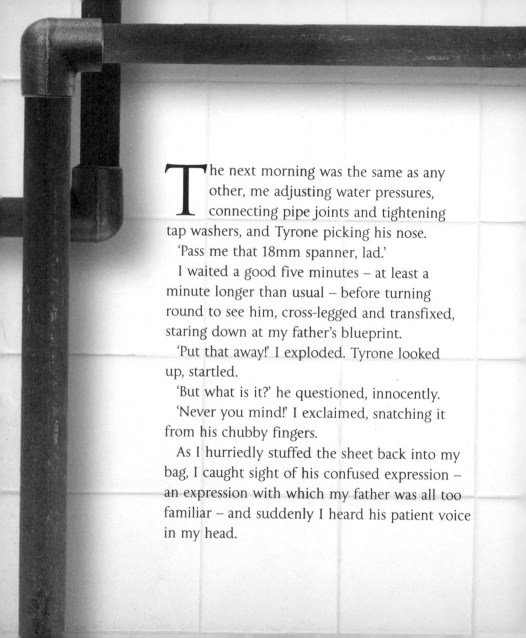

The next morning was the same as any other, me adjusting water pressures, connecting pipe joints and tightening tap washers, and Tyrone picking his nose.

'Pass me that 18mm spanner, lad.'

I waited a good five minutes – at least a minute longer than usual – before turning round to see him, cross-legged and transfixed, staring down at my father's blueprint.

'Put that away!' I exploded. Tyrone looked up, startled.

'But what is it?' he questioned, innocently.

'Never you mind!' I exclaimed, snatching it from his chubby fingers.

As I hurriedly stuffed the sheet back into my bag, I caught sight of his confused expression – an expression with which my father was all too familiar – and suddenly I heard his patient voice in my head.

'It is the duty of the elder to pass on his know-how to the younger.'

So I sat down beside the poor, hapless boy and told him everything.

'The Iron Throne?' he said, his eyes alight with wonder. 'My uncle has told me of this mythical toilet, but I never believed it really existed.'

'It doesn't,' I replied, lowering my head. 'Not anymore.'

'So what are you doing with the plans, are you going to build another?' he enquired, casting a glance at my spanner bag.

I shook my head firmly.

'But why not? The Iron Throne 2! A design like that would be sure to win the Golden Plunger!'

I hesitated. The Golden Plunger... My father's dream. If I could only recreate and somehow refine his idea, I could enter it in the annual Great Lavatory Exhibition and maybe win it for him. But no, that was just a pipe dream.

'That's enough of that nonsense, lad,' I said firmly. 'We'll say no more about it.'

Chastened, Tyrone sat in silence for a few minutes before slowly raising his head to look at me and utter the words that would change the rest of my life.

'An unhonoured father is like a bacon sandwich without ketchup.'

From that moment, I knew what I had to do. It would be a long and perilous journey, but one I had to take...

The sun splintered the dawn sky with golden shafts of light, angels burst into a heavenly chorus and suddenly I felt at one with the universe, both deeply relaxed and completely enlightened.

There's nothing quite like that first dump of the day.

Behind the closed door they stood huddled in the shadows, conspiring and plotting to kill me.

At least, I assume that's why women always go to the toilet in pairs . . .

We crossed the drawbridge
and were escorted by two guards
across the vast tree-lined courtyard,
through the gold-ceilinged great
hall, down the long mirrored
corridor and up the winding
diamond staircase to the top of the
Western tower. It was always a bit
of a palaver doing a plumbing
job for the Beckhams.

I stared in horror at the
hideous mess of limbs
and torsos. It was so bad
you could scarcely make out
which head belonged to
which body. But I still stuck
it on the fridge with my
daughter's other pictures.

I gazed, spellbound, as
she gyrated, shimmied and
squirmed before my eyes.

In the end I had no choice
but to let her use the
toilet before me.

'Get down on your knees, ladies. I want to see you do something really dirty together,' he commanded, as the two women trembled before him, their eyes cast downward. 'This toilet floor's too much work for one of you.'

The months came and went. Barbara's dragon collection was now over 200 and when she wasn't glued to her favourite TV show, she was spending more and more time with the neighbours. Meanwhile, I was spending every spare minute in the garden shed, hammering, sawing and soldering, often long into the night.

I have to admit that, with Karl and Delandra's hot tub being just the other side of the fence, I was a bit concerned about the constant banging, but with my earplugs in I was able to continue undisturbed. At last, the Iron Throne 2 was nearing completion and the Great Lavatory Exhibition was only days away, but I was still no nearer to remedying the fatal flaw of its predecessor.

Then, just as I was beginning to give up hope of ever restoring my father's legacy, the shed door burst open to reveal Barbara's face, glowing and moist from Jeremy's golden shower.

And in that moment I felt my life drain away. Never again would I see my friends' sad and smiley faces, or hear that sweet, sweet music. Goodbye to all my plans, my dreams – so many words left unsaid, so many things left undone. What a terrible, terrible waste! If only I hadn't dropped my iPhone down the toilet.

'I've had it up to here!' she cried.

I should have known, I suppose. The number of times I'd caught her thumbing through his glossy brochures. It was only a matter of time before her eye would be turned by his smoother, sleeker appliances.

'This isn't the life I wanted: you in this shed till all hours and me slaving away, taking care of our house and kids!'

'But...,' I began, wiping the sweat and grease from my brow.

'Don't you but me!' she retorted angrily. 'This obsession of yours is getting out of hand. Sometimes I think you love this big metal monstrosity more than me! You need to have a good think about your priorities, Graham.'

'I'm taking the kids off to Dragonland for the week and when I get back I want to see it gone! And while you're at it, sort that lock on the bathroom door. How on earth you managed to put it on the outside, I've no idea! And you can fix the blooming toilet handle too, so you don't have to flush it twice every time you go!'

With that, she headed off to Karl and Delandra's steam room and I sat heavily onto the iron seat. Deep down I knew she was right. I was as bad a husband and father as I was a plumber. I needed to listen to her more.

Now what was that she said about flushing twice...?

TRAPPED!

A prisoner within these four walls. I've tried everything – pushing, kicking and screaming for help, but still the door remains resolutely shut. Resigned to my fate, I reach deep inside my trousers and pull out the only thing that gives me comfort in times of great stress – **Practical Plumbing for Professionals**. The great, golden mystical bible for all water-based mechanics.

The musty yellowed tome falls open at an all-too-familiar page and my mind is instantly cast back to that fateful day many years ago...

The sight of her long golden tresses and glistening body being softly caressed by those gentle waves awoke a powerful urge inside me – I must replace the pump in that hot tub.

As I tentatively pushed the creaking door open, she swept swiftly around, arms waving wildly and shoved me away with the force of ten men.

'I'm sorry, dear. You'll have to use another cubicle. I'm still cleaning this one.'

I reeled backwards
from the sudden blow
to my face, my cheeks and
eyes stinging. I hate those
automatic air fresheners!

Suddenly there was a terrible roar and I felt like an invisible force was trying to tear my hands from my wrists. It was the first time I'd used a Dyson Airblade.

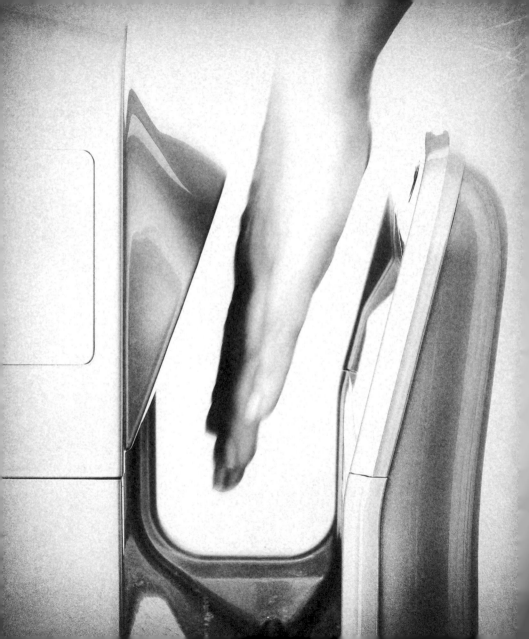

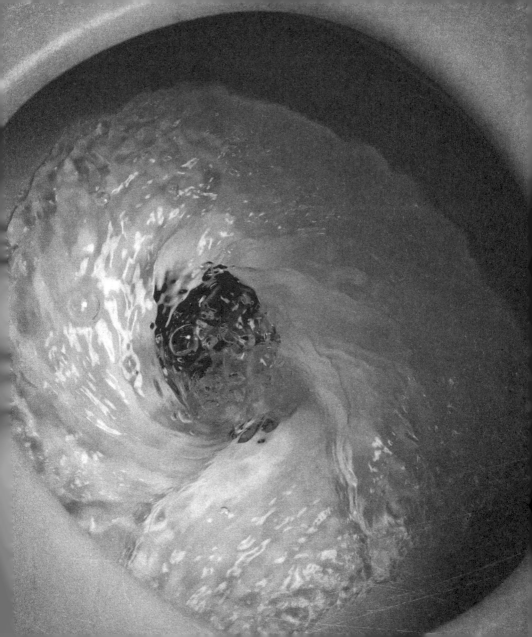

'This is madness!' I cried
in desperation.
'There must be an end to it!'

But no matter how much
I turned the toilet roll,
I couldn't find it.

I let my father's manual drop to the floor. How long have I been here? I glance at my watch. A quarter to seven! Only an hour until the Golden Plunger awards begin. I have to get out of here now! There's only one thing for it...

Somehow I manage to squeeze myself through the tiny bathroom window, scramble along the guttering and slide down the stack pipe, landing on the back patio with a resounding thud. I limp to the van, into which Tyrone and I had loaded the Iron Throne 2 the evening before, and set off down the A13 to face my destiny...

One hour, two speeding fines and a parking ticket later, I finally arrive at the tradesman's entrance to the central auditorium of the Great Lavatory Exhibition. Somehow, I'm going to have to find a way to shift my creation on my own, several calls to Tyrone's mobile having resulted in no more than the same garbled voicemail message:

'I'm sorry, Tyrone isn't available at the moment, he's busy eating a bacon sandwich.'

Sweating profusely and gasping for air, I rush to the back of the van and yank open the doors to see... Nothing!

Where is it? Where's the fruit of my last six months' labours? Six months that may have reclaimed my father's reputation, yet cost me my marriage. I frown and scratch my head frantically. Leaning wearily against the van door, my mind swirls round like an eleven Jet Trojan Cascade Whirlpool bath. Who could have taken it? And why?

Baffled and dizzied, I slowly make my way into the crowded exhibition hall just in time to hear the giant loudspeakers crackle into life and the announcer clear his throat.

'Ladies and Gents, after great deliberation and much straining on our seats, we have now arrived at the highlight of the evening's proceedings – the annual award for innovation in domestic lavatory design – the Golden Plunger!'

The auditorium bursts into expectant and enthusiastic applause. I sigh heavily. My chance to redeem my family's place in the annals of plumbing history has been flushed away like yesterday's lasagne. The announcer continues...

'This year has been an especially tough competition, with several notable number twos, but there can be only one number one. And this year that number one is an outstanding achievement, combining as it does the very best traditional lavatorial engineering with a unique futuristic vision – not only does it unblock itself, but you don't even need to leave your seat to flush it! Please put your spanners down and your hands together for the winner of the prestigious Golden Plunger award, seated on his magnificent creation!'

I can barely look as he wraps his hand round a long golden chain and proceeds to tug gently. The crimson velvet curtains glide slowly open to reveal, beneath a dazzling spotlight... a beaming, coiffured Jeremy Glennister, waving the plumber's holy grail triumphantly above his head, and sitting resplendently on... the Iron Throne 2! And standing uneasily beside him, a small sliver of bacon poking out of the corner of his mouth, his nephew Tyrone.

I stand in dumbfounded amazement and think back over the last year, my mind's eye trying to put the pieces of the jigsaw together. So Tyrone isn't the docile simpleton I'd taken him to be, after all! He's been spying for his uncle all along. Such treachery right beneath my nose!

The Glennisters must have deliberately locked me in the toilet to keep me away from the Great Lavatory Exhibition – and now my smug, self-satisfied neighbour has seized the throne!

I shake my head sadly as I realise my two fatal mistakes. One, naively trusting neighbours who have turned out to be my enemies. Two, putting the lock on the outside of the toilet door.

'And finally, Ladies and Gents, it's time to herald in the reign of our new king with the ceremonial flushing of the Toilet of the Year! Your Majesty, would you do us the pleasure?'

With a haughty grin, the wretched pretender to the throne grasps the ornate iron handle and yanks it firmly downward with a flourish...

Silence.

The audience stands, open-mouthed and expectant, until finally one small boy at the back of the room cries, 'Flush it again!'

Perturbed, Jeremy reaches once more for the handle and time seems to slow to a crawl. My mind flies back to that terrible day, all those years ago. My father's boots float before my eyes and my ears are filled with the unforgettable, haunting sound of that fatal second flush.

I realise in this moment that I'm the only one who knows the secret of the Iron Throne – to wait at least ten seconds for the turbo flush to engage successfully. And that a second flush would force the suction system to overload and switch to the hazardous emergency mode. Thank goodness I'm here! Just one word from me will save my neighbour from certain death...

EPILOGUE

Now, I sit here alone in my armchair, without my wife and without my children, reflecting on that day. So many times I've asked myself: did I do the right thing? And yet when I look at the photograph of my decent, honourable father beaming down proudly at me from the mantelpiece, I know in my heart that I did. And I smile wistfully, as my eyes lower to the hearth and his old boots, standing either side of the Golden Plunger.

ACKNOWLEDGEMENTS

We wish to express our boundless gratitude to the following brave warriors without whom this epic tale would have remained untold. Let their names be sung unto the very heavens by minstrels far and wide until the end of time...

Lord Ian R R Marshall of the houses of Simon & Schuster for leading us boldly into battle with a sure hand clasped firmly and constantly around his giant sword.

The venerable Nick R R Venables, wandering designer of repute and weaver of wondrous tapestries.

Sprightly Sir Matt R R Johnson, ironsmith and cover wrangler.

Lord Jamie R R Coleman of the houses of Greene and Heaton, protector of the royal purse and keeper of the royal beard.

Lord Armitage R R Shanks, a source of great comfort in troubled times.

And the once mighty clans of the North, South and Midlands – waifs, strays and vagabonds every one.

UNBOWED, UNBENT, UNBLOCKED.